I0441267

Mood Management Mastery

Learn How To Eliminate Negative Emotions To Gain Control Over Your Mind And Mood

Table of Contents

Introduction:...3

Chapter 1: Emotions and Self-Control.....................4

Chapter 2: When Emotionally Distressed: What
Impairs Self-Regulation?.....................................8

Chapter 3: Understanding Mood and Emotions........11

Chapter 4: Emotional and Moody: What Influences a
Person's Affectivity States?..............................12

Chapter 5: The Function of
Emotions...They......................15

Chapter 6: The Nature of Bad: Why the Negative is
Powerful?...16

Chapter 7: The Negative In Thinking.......................20

Chapter 8: The Automatic Negative Thoughts..........22

Chapter 9: Irrationalizing the Irrational: Challenging
the Negative Thoughts......................................29

Chapter 10: Dealing with Negative Thoughts and
Memories...35

Chapter 11: Acceptance and Moving On...................37

Chapter 12: Cultivating the Positive and Eliminating
the Negative...39

Conclusion...43

Introduction

I want to thank you and congratulate you for purchasing the book *Mood Management Mastery: Learn How to Eliminate Negative Emotions to Gain Control over Your Mind and Mood*.

This book contains proven steps and strategies on how to effectively deal with negative thoughts and bad memories. Also, the concepts of self-control, emotions and moods are all discussed in this book to help people better understand themselves.

Negative thoughts can cause misery and suffering. This is the reason why one must act quickly on such cognitive distortions. This book presents different ways to eliminate these negative ideas and cultivate positive thoughts and attitudes as replacements.

This book aims to give people a better understanding of all the significant concepts related to negative thoughts and healing. At the same time, this book helps people develop a holistic understanding of themselves as emotional and cognitive beings.

Thanks again for purchasing this book. I hope you enjoy it!

Chapter 1: Emotions and Self-Control

A person's ability to control himself starts developing during the very first year of life. With the development of self-control in relation to motor skills, cognition, and attention comes the development of the ability to control the expression of emotions. Every one of these developments is pivotal, but the capacity to control one's emotions holds a particular significance for the unfolding of adaptive and appropriate social behavior. A person with poorly developed control over emotions can be vulnerable to developing psychological issues.

Emotions, although regularly spoken about in everyday language, may are difficult to define. What most authors agree upon, however, is that emotions pertain to "a psychological state of specific duration that involves expressive behavior for communication." The importance of a person's ability to control his or her emotions has gradually been recognized over the past decade, particularly in developmental literature. Some studies involved understanding the factors that influence the development of self-control to manage emotions.

The way a person's emotional control develops can be influenced by several different factors. Some researchers label them intrinsic and extrinsic factors. One intrinsic factor is temperament. This refers to a child's reactivity to stimulation created by environment. Such reactivity is considered a somewhat stable trait of a child since it is present from the moment the child was born. How infants respond to environmental stimuli varies.

Experts believe the facial and vocal signs of negativity displayed by infants are due to generalized distress. Later in life, this develops into anger, sadness and fear. As the child's emotions develop, his or her cognition and self-awareness also unfolds. Consequently, the infant develops an ability to modulate his or her emotional reactivity.

Another intrinsic factor that influences the ability of a person to control his or her emotions is attention regulation. Just like temperament, the development of attention happens as early as the infant's first year of life. Attention refers to the ability to shift attention or sustain focus, and these are important to self-control development.

Inhibitory motor control is another factor that affects a person's self-control of emotions. Its development happens during the latter half of the infant's first year of life. Inhibitory motor control is the ability to stop a motor response.

Later on, the child learns to integrate his attention regulation and motor control. The successful integration of the two factors makes a child capable of managing his or her impulses and delaying gratification, which play significant roles later in life.

The emotional reactivity of each infant is unique, and such varying temperaments affect the development of the control processes mentioned above in equally varying ways.

While intrinsic factors play significant roles in the development of a person's self-control of emotions, other factors contribute largely to the process, as well. These factors are referred to as extrinsic aspects. Among the external factors, the quality of parenting holds the most value.

Indeed, the home is the child's first school. Here, the child learns to act and behave in accordance with a certain standard. The methods by which parents train their young ones and the kind of standards and expectations established in the home influence the child's development of emotional control. However, parenting style is also influenced by the child's temperament. For instance, studies reveal that temperamental infants have more intrusive mothers.

The parents' quality of interaction with the child and the child's temperament both affect one another. Hence, parents can shape their child's development. If the infant, for example, manages stress poorly, but the parents provided support, the child's sense of security will grow. Also, the child can learn to provide comfort to himself in such situations.

The relationship of parenting quality and the intrinsic factors of temperament and processes of control also relate in another way. One of the most valued assumptions is that parenting practices can either support or undermine the child's development. Children largely rely on their parents for behavioral and emotional support. Hence, this explains the maternal strategies of impulse inhibition and demand compliance as such powerful external regulators. It is also an expectation that such regulations become internalized by the child over time.

Parents model behaviors, including emotional regulation, to their children. Also, they act as the primary support when emotional control is needed.

In the family, the secondary emotional socializers are the siblings. Living together under the same roof and parental supervision for many or all of the developmental years, siblings have huge impacts on one another.

Another extrinsic factor that can influence a person's emotional control is peers and the peer environment. Because peers play a significant role in a person's life, they can also be a source of emotional support. Also, peers provide behavioral modeling when it comes to stressful circumstances.

On a larger scale, a person's emotional regulation development can be influenced by the cultural context he or she belongs to. The cultural standards will likely frame how a child displays or hides his or her emotions. Cultural influence is highly significant, because compliance to one's culture leads to social acceptance. Rules and norms governing the displays of emotions are directly passed through social institutions like family, school and church.

The ability to control one's emotions is far from a simple process. It is a product of several factors, both internal and external. The factors mentioned here are only some of the more important aspects that must be considered in understanding emotional control. Understanding these influential factors is necessary for understanding problems related to emotions and control.

Chapter 2: When Emotionally Distressed: What Impairs Self-Regulation?

The ability to self-regulate can offer several adaptive benefits. Being able to control one's emotions, impulse, behavior and desires is considered core to the human self. However, there are also several occasions where self-regulation fails. In most occasions, such deficiency of self-control is intertwined with different social and personal problems.

According to research, what lies beneath people's ability to self-regulate is their focus on long-term goals. However, at times of emotional distress, a person is compelled to change priorities and shift focus on the immediate present. Generally speaking, when a person experiences a bad feeling, he wants to feel better - and feel better immediately. Hence, the priority shifts from long-term goals to this short-term goal.

Impulsive acts used to escape emotional distress usually come with immediate pleasure. Consequently, while experiencing emotional distress, a person may prioritize feeling good (a short-term goal) and sacrifice his or her long-term goals in the process. This means impulse control and emotional regulation are intertwined.

Academic research has found that self-regulation, particularly impulse control, has the tendency to diminish when a person is experiencing emotional distress. For instance, studies showed that overweight people are likely to eat excessively when feeling depressed or anxious. This pattern is not limited to overweight and obese people. Even dieters, induced into a bad mood, displayed increased eating activity.

Several other studies found the same pattern when it comes to smoking and drinking activities. It is common for people to smoke more cigarettes and drink more alcoholic beverages when they are experiencing emotional distress. Also, self-control in activities like gambling and shopping fails with the presence of emotional troubles. Even the person's capacity to delay gratification cannot escape the influence of emotional distress. Distressed people are more likely to choose small, but immediate rewards over larger rewards that take more time to obtain.

Indeed, there is much academic evidence supporting the idea that self-regulation diminishes with emotional distress. However, what is rather unclear is why the pattern occurs. There are several theories offering explanation as to why distress impairs self-control.

According to one theory, a person undergoing emotional distress does not think rationally. Consequently, he is less likely to regulate his emotions properly. This is the reason why emotionally upset individuals turn impulsive, pre-occupied, and risk-oriented.

Another theory claims that an emotionally distraught person is inclined toward self-destructive tendencies. Hence, he is predisposed to abandoning desirable long-term goals and adaptive and healthy behaviors.

Another theory suggests that instead of directly impairing the self-regulation of a person, emotional distress is actually influencing the motivation of the person. There are three ways to interpret this theory. One is by considering apathy. A person experiencing emotional turmoil may suddenly feel indifferent toward pursuing a desirable and positive goal in life. Simply put, the person ceases to care. Thus, the person devotes no effort to regulating emotions.

The second way to interpret the theory concerns rebellion. A person experiencing emotional problems may turn rebellious and completely abandon appropriate behavior. Consequently, he thwarts his own regulation patterns.

Lastly, some believe an emotionally upset person can simply give up on his or her long-term goals due to a feeling of incapability. Thus, the person is more likely to focus only on his short-term objectives. This is the self-efficacy version.

Several other theories try to shed light on why emotional distress can impair emotional self-regulation. Although the possibilities are numerous, current knowledge on the subject can suffice in helping a person make sense of the complexity of emotions and control, in general.

Chapter 3: Understanding Mood and Emotions

Affectivity is a broader heading that encompasses an extensive range of feelings that people experience. Affect, therefore, includes both emotions and mood. Although, the terms are interchangeably used, the two actually have different meanings. Emotions refer to feelings that are intense and directed at something or someone. Mood, on the other hand, talks about less intense feelings that usually lack context.

Most experts believe that emotions are more fleeting than mood. Emotions can quickly change from angry to sad to happy, but when it comes to mood, it can last for hours or days. Mood, unlike emotions, do not usually focus on a specific person, thing or event. The two states of affectivity, nevertheless, can influence one another. Emotions can give rise to a certain mood, and mood can make a person more emotional.

Mood is less clear than emotions. There are only two categories for mood, namely, positive and negative mood. Conversely, emotions have very specific in terms like anger, sadness, happiness, fear and so on. What causes mood changes is general and unclear, while what causes emotional shifts is usually specific and obvious.

Chapter 4: Emotional and Moody: What Influences a Person's Affectivity States?

There are many internal factors influencing a person's affectivity. Also, a person's affect is highly vulnerable to the impacts of outside forces. What puts a person in a good or bad mood or makes him feel mad or happy does not fall on a single factor but rather a combination of intrinsic and extrinsic influences. Identifying these factors is important for helping a person better understand his emotional states and mood shifts.

One major factor that influences a person's affect is his personality. No two people have exactly the same personality. Some books even describe it as the factor that makes each individual unique. Personality gives a person his inimitable way of seeing things, understanding events and experiencing emotional states.

Every human being feels both physically and emotionally. However, it is apparent that each individual has different ways of expressing their emotions. Also, different people have varying threshold for emotional pain. In the everyday life, it is common to encounter people who readily lose their tempers for minor reasons and other people who seem unwaveringly kind. Indeed, some people have a natural inclination to feel more intense emotions than others. While some may cry out loud at a sad film, others may just feel sad about it.

Stress is another factor that can largely influence a person's mood and emotions. For instance, a forthcoming deadline or a reprimand from superiors at work can induce negative moods and unpleasant emotions in an employee. As mentioned earlier, mood lasts longer than emotions. Hence, it is common for a working mother or father to bring home a stressed out mood after work. Because a bad mood lasts longer than anger or fear, it is more likely for the person to experience another bad work day the following day. One must be watchful of stress because it builds up over time.

"Thank God it's Friday!" The popularity of this cliché can be explained by the next factor that can impact a person's emotional states and mood: the day of the week. Research reveals that people experience the height of negative mood at the beginning of the week. Positive moods, on the other hand, were found highest at the end of the week.

In addition, studies also reveal that people's mood and emotions are influenced by the time of the day. Most people are low-spirited during morning and feel better mid-day, and then the mood declines in the evening. This information can help a person spot the perfect time to ask a friend for a favor or to identify when to break bad news.

Another factor that has significant influence on a person's mood is the social activities he participates in. Social activities have little effect on people's negative moods, but they increase people's good moods significantly. Furthermore, research reveals that informal and physical activities induce positive moods more effectively than formal or sedentary events.

The next factor that must be considered is sleep. Sleep-deprived people are prone to experiencing intense anger, fatigue and hostility. Lack of good quality sleep is associated with poor mood mainly because it makes emotional regulation difficult and impairs a person's decision-making skills.

One major external factor that can greatly influence a person's emotion and mood is culture. People from different cultures generally interpret pleasant and unpleasant emotions in similar manner. For instance, anger is bad and happiness is good across all cultures. However, the degree of valuation and specific interpretation may differ with certain emotions. Consider pride as an example. Western countries take this as a positive feeling, but for Eastern countries like Japan and China, this is viewed as an undesirable trait.

The way people express their emotions varies, as well. In individualistic countries, a person's display of emotions is not seen as directed toward the person he is communicating with. Nevertheless, for collectivist countries, the opposite holds true. The relationship of the two people communicating is greatly affects the types of emotions expressed and the way they are expressed.

These factors are just some of the major aspects that can influence a person's emotions and mood. Aside from better understanding his emotional states, identifying these influences can also help a person formulate appropriate solutions in case emotional problems arise.

Chapter 5: The Function of Emotions

According to Charles Darwin's book, *The Expression of the Emotions in Man and Animals,* people develop emotions over time because it is necessary for problem-solving. Emotions, Darwin said, are the motivators that push people to pursue actions necessary for survival. For instance, disgust causes one to avoid potentially harmful things like rotten food.

Today, evolutionary psychology is now the field of science following Darwin's perspective. According to this field, people must experience both positive and negative emotions because they serve certain purposes.

For instance, anger can be seen as generally bad. Nevertheless, it actually helps people guard their rights. A person who was deceived by a friend may display his or her anger, and such emotional expression serves as a demand that other people not commit the same act against him again.

Although the explanations provided by the evolutionary psychology seem highly probable, other psychologists still see loopholes with the evolutionary perspective. Until now, it is still unclear whether the said perspective is true across varying circumstances. What is clear, though, is that emotions significantly influence a person. Emotions contain a significant amount of power that could make or break a person.

Chapter 6: The Nature of Bad: Why the Negative is Powerful?

The bad is more powerful than the good, which is the notion that some researchers support. In several different aspects of human life, many believe that negative events impact a person more than positive events. For instance, studies reveal that negative or traumatic life events wear off much more slowly than positive events.

One study assessed the happiness of three groups. The first group consisted of lottery winners who won a year prior the interview. The second group contained people who became paralyzed after an accident one year earlier. The last group included people who did not experience any major life event in the past year. The results revealed that the lottery winners did not experience any more happiness than the other two groups.

As the authors explained it, the lottery winners experienced a short-lived euphoria of good fortune. After the experience of euphoria, the level of happiness of the lottery winners went back to the level prior to winning. It was also noted that the only lasting effect of winning the lottery was the decreased enjoyment in ordinary pleasures, which is a negative aspect of winning the lottery.

The group who experienced an accident, however, showed a slower adaptation to the changes in their lives. According to the study, they were significantly less happy than the other groups, mainly because they developed a habit of continuously comparing their lives before and after the accident.

In the developmental field of psychology, it was likewise observed that a bad event outweighs a good event. Several studies revealed that child abuse (sexual or physical) has long-term and harmful consequences. Even if the abuse took place only once or twice, such a negative experience is powerful enough to make the person highly vulnerable to depression, sexual dysfunction, relationship problems, or becoming a victim again. In addition to this, several studies could not prove that any positive experience had the power to offset the negative consequences of the experienced abuse.

Even in the assessment of people's everyday experiences, studies maintained the idea that the bad is more powerful than the good. One study showed that everyday good and bad events can significantly influence a person's subsequent mood. Nonetheless, the bad or negative experiences created more invasive effects on the person's mood. It was further revealed that negative events affect a person's good and bad mood, while a positive event only influences a good mood.

A separate study assessed the duration of the effects of both bad and good events on a person. The longer lasting effects were caused by bad events. According to the study, it was likely for a person to have a lower level of wellbeing following a bad day. A good day, however, did not carry over any influence on the next day.

In relation to emotions, studies used language to determine which emotion, bad (unpleasant) or good (pleasant), is more powerful. It was revealed from different studies that negative emotions are more fully represented in the language than positive ones. In another study, participants from six countries were asked to list all the emotion words they could think of in five minutes.

When the researchers tallied the result, words like fear, anger, joy and sadness were the common answers from all six countries that made the top 12. This also suggests that people find it more significant to label negative emotions than positive ones.

The study regarding emotional regulation also confirms the hypothesis that negative emotions hold more power than positive emotions. When people try changing their moods, they resort to certain techniques to do so. The study reveals that people have developed more techniques to avoid unpleasant emotions than to induce pleasant emotions. Since negative emotions take more effort and time to avoid, this supports the notion that negative emotional states hold consequential power.

Several other studies arrived at the same conclusion that the bad has power beyond that of the good. In almost every aspect of human life, it seems that people are more sensitive and responsive to negative information. The lasting effects of negative experiences or relationships may occur because the learned lessons from the experiences are needed to prevent the same danger in the future. As for good experience or emotions, they appear to wear off rather easily because of humans' predispositions to seek for better experience every time.

While the idea that negative events and emotions have more strength than their positive counterparts may feel disparaging, the affects of negative events can have powerful yet positive effects. It is important to note that studies claim the good or the positive cannot usually defeat the stronger bad or negative. According to experts, the good can defeat the bad in numbers, though. Gottman (1994) said that the ratio is five goods, at least, for every bad. Hence, people must concentrate on doing more positive acts and celebrating successes no matter how small.

Chapter 7: The Negative In Thinking

The previous chapter discussed the power of the negative in relation to the different aspects of the human life. Now the discussion will narrow down to a rather specific field – that is, human thinking.

People experience numerous psychological challenges that stem from negative thinking. Most of the time, the problem does not lie in the situation but in the more powerful factor of the human mind. Indeed, it is very common for people to create their own negativities that bring about stress, which only furthers negativity in their lives.

As mentioned earlier, negative thoughts linger longer in a person's consciousness, making him more vigilant to threats or dangers similar to the one previously experienced. Consequently, it is common for the negative thoughts to trigger easily, as they usually lay dormant in the person's mind. Some negative thoughts are obvious and known to the person holding them. However, some unpleasant thoughts can be vague and may even work without the knowledge of the person.

There is no effort necessary for negative thoughts to occur in a person's mind. Commonly, they seem to appear automatically. For this reason, they are commonly labeled as "automatic negative thoughts." These unpleasant thoughts usually attack a person's mind while his mind is in a neutral state. Automatic negative thoughts feel true to the thinker, so they usually have significant power over the person. Nevertheless, in reality, negative thoughts rarely hold much truth. Such thoughts usually exaggerate and distort reality, particularly if a stressful life event triggers them

Chapter 8: The Automatic Negative Thoughts

Several unpleasant ways of thinking distort the perception of a person's reality. The power of negative thoughts is undeniable, and it can make a person less capable of adapting to his social environment. As mentioned earlier, some of the negative thoughts appear less obvious than others. Hence, the types of automatic negative thoughts commonly experienced by people are listed here:

The first type describes *absolute pessimism*. This type of thinking concentrates solely on the negative aspects of life, events, people or situations. The excessive amount of attention given to the negative side completely hides the positive aspects, which are very much present. Such thinking makes a person focus on his negative qualities, while ignoring the positive traits at the same time. Even if a person receives compliments or recognition, he still thinks such positive outcomes do not count.

The second illogical way of thinking is *overgeneralization*. People commonly use terms that over generalize a situation, such as *everything, anything, all, no one,* and *never* when they make statements about themselves or others during times of heightened emotions. For instance, a person suffering from depression may say he cannot do *anything* right. Overgeneralizing is the kind of thinking that removes any positive possibilities based on one instance of failure. A person who failed to learn a few dance steps, for example, may claim that he or she is not good at *anything* at *all.* By removing even the slightest chance to perform better or do something well, a person embraces defeat before he or she even starts fighting.

The third cognitive distortion is known as *disqualifying the positives*. This describes the person's predisposition to discard his achievement before he or she starts feeling its positive effects. It is a common experience for people to disregard the positive things happening in their lives. The rewarding feeling eventually wears off, and the satisfaction from the positive experience no longer elicits the same excitement or appreciation from the person. This kind of thinking can simply be described as a "so what" kind of attitude. The danger of this cognitive distortion lies in the reduction of pleasure one feels in life.

The fourth automatic negative thought is called *exaggerating*. This kind of thinking distorts reality by inappropriately magnifying a single event. For instance, a person received a minor criticism from his superior about the presentation he used during the meeting. When the meeting ended, the person felt terrible and told a friend that the boss did not like his ideas at all. This particular kind of thinking can be dangerous, particularly in relationships.

When exaggerations about events and people, an extreme view of an event's consequences, and intense fear are linked together, catastrophizing may take place. This is another kind of thinking that makes a person imagine several unwanted consequences from a seemingly harmless event.

For instance, a person received a letter from a legal office. From the moment he laid his eyes on the sender information on the envelope, he started imagining being the subject of a lawsuit, followed by the assumption that he would land in jail in no time. He then imagined his family abandoning him because of the shame he brought them.

He further thought his family would never visit him, and this would leave him depressed with no choice except suicide in his cold cell. These thoughts frightened him to the point that he decided not to open the letter. After a couple dreadful days, he finally read the letter and found out his grandmother willed him a small fortune.

This example appears to be an extreme one, but it clearly depicts catastrophizing. This thinking commonly occurs in people suffering from depression or anxiety disorders.

The fourth kind of illogical thinking is called *all-or-nothing* thinking. This kind of distorted thinking makes a person see things in black and white. Indeed, there are no gray areas for such a mindset. When a person only sees an event as good or bad, he loses his ability to adapt properly. People who view situations on a spectrum of good and bad are comparably more adaptable. Some people focus on their high goals, and if they fall short of them, they already consider themselves failures. For a person who thinks in an all-or-nothing way, the rules are rigid, and flexibility or consideration is not an option.

The fifth cognitive distortion is the use of *"should" statements*. This kind of thinking involves the moral issues of things, events or people. The use of "should" or "ought to" in statements gives a kind of automatic judgment to the subject. If the should statement is directed at oneself, it can easily stir feelings of inadequacy or guilt. *"I should have done better than that." "I should have perfected the examination." "I should have loved him/her better."* These statements give a person the feeling that he failed to do something properly.

When the statements are directed at other people, the statement creates the impression of others being bad, inconsiderate or terrible. *"She should have prepared healthier food for her children." "He should have considered not breaking up with her over the phone." "They should have dressed better for the occasion."* Such statements readily label people in a negative manner. It turns into a judgment if the person is looking at the action out of its context. The problem with the "should" statement is not the word itself. Rather, the issue is the appropriate use of a term as powerful as "should" or "ought." Using should statements in discussing moral issues in life is more accurate. Matters like stealing or killing are the kind of issues where *should* and *should not* is more fitting.

The sixth automatic negative thinking is known as *mindreading.* Humans can be intuitive at times, and there are several instances when they rely heavily on their intuition to assess events in their life. Mindreading, in this case, is the person's pre-conception of what another person is thinking about. This, however, is not based on any evidence that would justify the judgment. This kind of thinking is troublesome because is a chance the person could misread the actions or words of another. This can lead to a ruined relationship and more maladaptive behaviors for the one doing the guesswork.

The seventh kind of negative thought is also characterized by jumping to conclusions. This kind of thinking is called *fortunetelling*. While mindreading assumes the thoughts of others, fortunetelling creates immediate conclusions that are, most of the time, bad endings. This fortunetelling is associated with self-fulfilling prophecy. Sometimes, what people expect from events or situations comes true because they base their behaviors on the expected result.

For instance, two girls are all alone in a classroom. Jill is really the silent type while Anne is a very popular kid in school. The awkward silence inside the room makes both of them want to break it by talking to another. However, something kept them from doing so. Jill thinks that Anne is too popular to want to talk to someone like her. Hence, she pretended to read a book. Meanwhile, Anne was actually thinking of opening a conversation with Jill. However, when she saw Jill reading, she thought Jill was busy and uninterested in talking with her. Thus, she just started listening to the music from her iPod. Both of the girls closed their communication channels, and by doing so, they are both fulfilling their own prophecy that the other is not interested in conversation.

The same happens when a man who was invited to a party thinks he will feel out of place with the crowd. He readily assumed that no one in the party would even talk to him. Hence, while at the said party, he acted distant to other people because of the negative expectation in his mind. In turn, no one approached him the entire night.

Self-fulfilling prophecy and fortunetelling in general can be very convincing. Hence, the person never realized that the negative thoughts greatly influenced his displayed behavior. This, in turn, caused other people to elicit behaviors he or she was expected from the beginning.

The eighth kind of automatic negative thinking is the "*what if's*" and "*if only's.*" This kind of thinking favors the option the person failed to choose in the past. Moreover, this kind of thinking assumes the other option could have led to a better result. Consequently, the person is weakening his self-trust when it comes to decision-making processes.

The ninth cognitive distortion is called *emotional reasoning*. This is the kind of thinking where people base their thoughts on emotions. For people suffering from depression, the *feeling* that they are worthless is very common. Nevertheless, it cannot be true that a person does not amount to anything. As mentioned in the previous chapters, emotions can be powerful enough to cloud a person's rational thinking. Consequently, reasoning crafted out of emotions may be unreliable due to its lack of logic.

Labeling is the tenth negative pattern of thinking. This depicts a person's inclination to label himself in the most undesirable way possible. For instance, a person having a hard time recalling something labels himself "stupid." There can be several factors influencing such criticisms. One factor could be that the person was imitating what his parents used to call him.

Lastly, people have negative thoughts in the form of *personalization*. This kind of thinking makes a person think that a certain event or situation involves him in a major way, even if it does not in reality. Personalization centers every issue on oneself. It is similar to the spotlight effect, which describes a person's feeling that he is always under the spotlight. It is a common feeling people experience when they step into a party, and the world seems to move slowly as he feels everyone looking at him. With personalization, however, the experience is rather negative. Whenever a friend is angry, the boss is upset or a project proposal was denied, the person personalizing considers himself as the reason for such troubles.

There is no doubt that thoughts influence one's feelings and actions. If one thinks that nothing right will happen, he or she will feel sad and will end up not trying to do anything at all. Someone who thinks that he or she is unlikable will feel like an outcast in any situation. He or she will be disappointed and will withdraw socially. Such connection linking thoughts, feelings and behaviors together makes negative thinking rather dangerous. Consequently, one has to act upon negative thoughts before they breed and take complete control of their lives.

Chapter 9: Irrationalizing the Irrational: Challenging the Negative Thoughts

Most of the time, the problems people suffer from come from their minds and not from reality. As previously discussed, there are several negative thoughts that can automatically pop into someone's head, bending reality for the person. Irrational thoughts can transform regular disappointment into something awful. This can make a person less functional in major areas of his life. Since the problem is in the person's way of thinking, then the solution must revolve around changing his or her way of thinking.

The fact that the problem lies in the human mind makes it difficult and easy to deal with, depending on how it is looked at. It is difficult in the sense that negative thinking practiced for a long time cannot be changed quickly. It might require a lot of time before a person can consider himself free of the influences of such unwanted thoughts. Time, however, is a luxury some people do not have. Patience is gold and some people are still mining for a piece. Nevertheless, solving problems with negative thoughts is also easy. This is because the solution for this problem does not require a person to move mountains. The person is the one in control of his or her mind, so the person actually has direct control over the issue.

The very first step in combating destructive negative thoughts is identifying them. This is the basic step necessary for most human problems. Only by knowing the problem can a person develop the necessary plan of action to eliminate it. As mentioned in the previous discussion, there are several negative and irrational thoughts that breed in people's minds. They can take different forms and can impact the person's functioning in varying degrees.

At present, it is believed by experts that there are actually thousands of false ideas that cause misery to people. Some of these can be subtle but so convincing, and others are rather obvious and bold. Hence, a person must observe his or her own way of thinking for a certain period of time. In the previous chapter, 11 of the illogical ways of thinking were discussed, and one can use that list as a guide to decipher his or her unwanted thoughts. Writing every thought observed is necessary. Negative thoughts tend to storm a person's mind, so one can easily lose track of them if they are not jotted down accordingly.

Nonetheless, one should not expect this step to come easily. There are several irrational thoughts the person must have repeatedly experiences to the point that the thoughts became fact to the person.

The next step is identifying the factors that trigger negative thoughts. This can be done by listing the times and circumstances where the negative thought surfaced. Also, one must list the exact feelings that could have generated the unwanted cognitive distortion. Subtle thoughts can be difficult to pinpoint, but by identifying undesirable emotions, one can improve chances of uncovering the underlying illogical idea.

Following this step is the assessment of the possible evidence of the thoughts listed. For instance, a person feels like he is not good at anything at all. Then, the person must write down all the activities he performs satisfactorily or even exceptionally. It is easier to convince the mind to let go of a belief if the evidence disproving the belief are very clear.

Next is to dispute the disruptive negative thoughts. Challenging an illogical way of thinking can take the form of exploring different interpretations of a seemingly upsetting event. For instance, a project proposal made by Mary was rejected by her boss. She felt so bad that she started thinking her boss had never liked her. Instead of dwelling on such a negative interpretation of what happened, Mary must consider other possible interpretations of the situation. It is possible that Mary's boss was only trying to motivate her to give her best in her job. Her boss, perhaps, has seen her better performances at work, and he wanted her to be at her best always.

The event can also be interpreted as Mary's learning opportunity. Experience is the best teacher, after all. By experiencing rejection first hand, Mary became knowledgeable on what to do and not do in order to be successful in the future. It is also possible that her project proposal was out of the budget range of the company. There are several ways to interpret a single event. Hence, it is illogical to stick with the worst or most undesirable possibility.

A person can debate against his or her own negative thoughts. Effective arguments against the cognitive distortions can be created once the person has a full understanding of the ramifications of these thoughts. By continuously asking the question, "Why?" to oneself, a person can discover more of his impossible demands on himself. At the same time, he or she can see the pattern of his or her distorted reasoning.

Some people are fond of labeling themselves with put-downs. Luckily, there is also a way to turn that habit into something healthy for the self. By restating the negative labels as positive ones, a person can feel better about himself. For instance, the term lazy can be replaced with the words relaxed or carefree.

The next step is creating rational statements to replace the irrational ones listed. Consider the following examples.

I must always perfect the school examinations. If I fail to do so, then I am nothing but a failure. Making mistakes is unacceptable. (Irrational thought)

No one is perfect. Everyone has his or her own weakness. Committing mistakes is a common feature of every individual. Failures, mistakes and faults are all part of the learning process. Only through learning can a person become better. (Rational thinking)

I do not want to try anything. I always fail anyway! (Irrational thinking)

I cannot tell what the outcome of this activity will be. I can succeed at this or I can fail. Either way, I win, for this is a new learning experience for me, a kind of experience that is rewarding in itself. Indeed, I cannot control the outcome, but I can control how hard I try. (Rational thinking)

By exploring rational thoughts to counter the prevailing illogical ideas, one frees his mind to consider other possibilities. This is a good start to alter the negative pattern of thinking and to change it using a healthier positive ways of looking at things.

Self-talk can also help in eliminating negative thoughts gradually. However, one must be careful about the content of his self-talk. The power of self-talk lies in the repetition of the idea to the self. The mind has an inclination to believe an idea that is usually present in the person's consciousness, so repetition works well to embed a belief in the mind.

The aim of self-talk is to support a healthier self. Thus, one must avoid halting ideas like, "Don't be emotional" or, "Always be perfect." Instead, one must use self-talk containing allowing messages like, "It is always okay to make mistakes," and, "Nothing is wrong with being emotional. I am a human being capable of feeling, and I have to respect that."

The last step is to be mindful of the occurrence of any negative thought, and attack it immediately before it starts building up. Remember, however, that this method is only effective with repetitive practice. Indeed, negative thoughts can surface anytime of the day, so being alert to these unpleasant ideas is the best way to combat such negative thinking.

Another important consideration to remember is that immediate result cannot be expected. As mentioned earlier, it takes time to eliminate negative ways of thinking. Hence, the techniques and steps mentioned above must be practiced for as long as needed. What is certain is that changing the negative thoughts to positive ones is highly doable. Logical reasoning, however, is hard work. Being rational requires a lifetime commitment. Consequently, some people leave the job undone by giving up early before anything is accomplished.

Chapter 10: Dealing with Negative Thoughts and Memories

As discussed in the previous chapter, bad memories and unpleasant thoughts affect a person longer than positive ones. This makes a lot of people suffer with repetitive negative thoughts and negative experiences of the past.

In the academic scene, experts do not agree on the most effective means of dealing with negative memories and thoughts. Using the psychoanalytic perspective (pioneered by Sigmund Freud), disturbing emotions must be expressed. For this school of thought, there is no other way for a person to effectively combat unwanted memories except by talking about it – even if it requires a person to dig the bad memory out of his or her unconscious mind.

People have a natural inclination to repress their bad memories. They try to hide them in the deepest part of their brain. However, this is an ineffective way of dealing with such memories. According to psychotherapists, the repressed memories act like a toxin and seep out in more problematic forms like psychological disorders.

However, some research supports the claim that repressing a bad memory actually facilitates forgetting. Once the person has forgotten an unwanted past experience, then there is no way the memory can have negative effects. Nevertheless, this idea needs more research support because most therapy still focuses on decreasing the repression of undesirable memories.

Contrary to this, another research claims that people who deliberately avoid their negative thoughts or bad memories are not making any progress. Instead, they are making the situation worse. The said study revealed that more uncontrollable negative thoughts will be produced by a person who opts to not talk about bad memories. It is likened to what happens if one is asked not to think of a monkey for the next five minutes.

Indeed, science is still on its way to find the best way for people to manage undesirable memories and thoughts. As of now, there are different approaches suggested by various studies that are worthy of trying. Consequently, a person must try the methods to see which works best.

Chapter 11: Acceptance and Moving On

While there are people obsessing over their bad memories or negative thoughts, others enjoy life without trying to forget about their undesirable past experience. It is highly possible that two individuals remember the same event in totally different ways. Individual differences when it comes to perception and the unreliability of the human memory are some factors that could cause such difference in interpretation.

While researchers are still trying to find the best way to deal with this problem, one could start by changing factors within his control. A person's acceptance is a helpful way to effectively deal with unwanted memories. Before one can forget or dig up bad memories, he must first learn to accept it. It could be that a person is continuously bothered by bad memories because a part of him is still resisting the negativity of the event.

With acceptance, a person recognizes that the bad experience took place and that it was indeed painful. A person must accept that the experience affected his life both in negative and positive ways. Most importantly, a person must accept that it is now all over. The experience is in a distant past far from where he is right now. A person must realize that moving on from that negative experience, regardless of how difficult it is, means he is strong enough to carry on with life. A person must accept that he cannot go back to the past. One cannot heal the wounds in the past for that is the task of the present. and the future is for a new beginning.

Bad memories, perhaps, can be likened to a wound. One does not need to rush its healing for it will eventually heal itself naturally. Time really heals, but one must be very patient. What matters is that the person recognizes that the wound exists and is now a part of him. Whether he opts to talk about it or to forget about it, the wound, the memory, the experience is still there. Soon, the wound leaves a scar, and it is up to the person if he sees it as a scar of defeat or a scar of triumph.

Chapter 12: Cultivating the Positive and Eliminating the Negative

It is amazing how people can respond so differently to the same situation. The exact same stimulus can make different people elicit varying responses. Aside from what was previously discussed, attitude is another factor responsible for individual differences in response. Thoughts, attitudes and behavior can influence one another.

Attitude can be better understood by looking at its ABC components – that is, affectivity, behavioral and cognitive parts. Affectivity is the evaluative part, and it describes a person's feelings about a certain situation, event or person. The behavioral part is the overt response or action taken, and the cognitive aspect talks about what a person thinks, knows or believes about a person or event. Changing one of these components can change the other two. Attitude is dynamic, and it can influence a person's thoughts. Consequently, cultivating a positive attitude can help improve a person's way of thinking.

The first step to improve one's attitude is to be aware of the current attitude. This is possible through self-observation. One can tell if he is more of an optimist or pessimist or whether he is introverted or extroverted through this process. Friends and family can also help a person assess his behavior by sharing what they see in him. There are also scales and tests that give one an objective description of his attitude.

A person with a clear attitude can avoid the phenomenon of cognitive dissonance. This describes a person's predisposition to act and think in opposite manners. If it is clear to a person how he sees, feels and thinks about a certain issue, he can display behaviors parallel to what he believes in.

The second step is to identify desired the positive attitude. A particular attitude that several researches support is optimism. This attitude describes a person's hopefulness and high expectation of the future. Such attitude of hope and positive orientation can protect a person from psychological distress. It is revealed by several studies that having an optimistic attitude betters a person's mental and physical health. In addition to this, optimism was found to be a necessary ingredient for success in almost all aspects of human life.

For instance, a person who thinks negatively of himself always pulls back and avoids trying new things. Consequently, his potentials, skills and talents remain unexplored and underutilized, making him an underachiever for his entire life.

Optimism is commonly mistaken as a kind of attitude that is cheerful no matter what happens. Healthy optimism is not like that. Positive thinkers never deny the existence of their problems, and yes, they do experience problems. They are simply open and ready to address problems in however they can. Optimistic individuals respond actively to their lives, as they are aware that what they do shapes their future.

The third step is to start developing the desired positive attitude. If a person wants to be optimistic, then he or she should practice the attitude. Optimism is not just about being happy all the time. One must learn to face problems and even expect bad times with the aim of solving the issue. Keeping an open mind about the possible solutions is a habit of optimistic individuals. What makes positive thinkers appear constantly cheerful is the fact that they never fail to see the good even in the worst situation. Indeed, being optimistic requires looking at the bright side instead of the depressing part.

To be optimistic means a person is not defeated by his or her negative thoughts. Instead, the person is actively challenging irrational thoughts and is replacing unpleasant ideas with pleasing ones. An optimist also knows how to appreciate life. This gives the person a lighter perspective in life. An optimist is grateful and appreciative even of the rain. No matter how big or small the good in a situation is, the optimist sees it and appreciates it.

Optimism makes a person able to laugh and celebrate life even in the toughest situations. An optimistic person has the ability to control himself. Hence, he or she can adapt better to various circumstances. Accepting that there are things people cannot change is another practice of optimists. Consequently, the optimist rarely complains as he decided not to focus on things beyond his control. What the optimist focuses on instead are his ways of seeing things, manners of performing his tasks, polishing his skills, renewing his energy and spirit, and all that is within his power.

Practicing these specific attitudinal inclinations helps a person cultivate the positive and eliminate the negative.

Conclusion

Thank you again for purchasing this book!

I hope this book helped you understand and address your problems of repetitive negative thoughts and bad memories.

The next step is to apply the steps and techniques mentioned in this book and to share this information with your friends and family.

Thank you and good luck!

www.ingramcontent.com/pod-product-compliance
Lightning Source LLC
Chambersburg PA
CBHW070843310526
45793CB00011B/523